# BORN-AGAIN BELIEVERS
Evangelicals & Charismatics

# RELIGION & MODERN CULTURE
## Title List

# BORN-AGAIN BELIEVERS
## Evangelicals & Charismatics

by Kenneth McIntosh, M.Div.,
and Marsha McIntosh

Mason Crest Publishers
Philadelphia

Mason Crest Publishers Inc.
370 Reed Road
Broomall, Pennsylvania 19008
(866) MCP-BOOK (toll free)

First printing
1 2 3 4 5 6 7 8 9 10

Library of Congress Cataloging-in-Publication Data

McIntosh, Kenneth, 1959–
  Born-again believers : evangelicals & charismatics / by Kenneth R. McIntosh and Marsha L. McIntosh.
      p. cm. — (Religion and modern culture)
  Includes index.
  ISBN 1-59084-974-4   ISBN 1-59084-970-1 (series)
  1.  Evangelicalism. 2.  Pentecostal churches.  I. McIntosh, Marsha. II. Title. III. Series.
  BR1640.M43 2006
  277.3'083—dc22

                                        2005014057

Produced by Harding House Publishing Service, Inc.
www.hardinghousepages.com
Interior design by Dianne Hodack.
Cover design by MK Bassett-Harvey.
Printed in India.

# CONTENTS

# INTRODUCTION

by Dr. Marcus J. Borg

You are about to begin an important and exciting experience: the study of modern religion. Knowing about religion—and religions—is vital for understanding our neighbors, whether they live down the street or across the globe.

Despite the modern trend toward religious doubt, most of the world's population continues to be religious. Of the approximately six billion people alive today, around two billion are Christians, one billion are Muslims, 800 million are Hindus, and 400 million are Buddhists. Smaller numbers are Sikhs, Shinto, Confucian, Taoist, Jewish, and indigenous religions.

Religion plays an especially important role in North America. The United States is the most religious country in the Western world: about 80 percent of Americans say that religion is "important" or "very important" to them. Around 95 percent say they believe in God. These figures are very different in Europe, where the percentages are much smaller. Canada is "in between": the figures are lower than for the United States, but significantly higher than in Europe. In Canada, 68 percent of citizens say religion is of "high importance," and 81 percent believe in God or a higher being.

The United States is largely Christian. Around 80 percent describe themselves as Christian. In Canada, professing Christians are 77 percent of the population. But religious diversity is growing. According to Harvard scholar Diana Eck's recent book *A New Religious America*, the United States has recently become the most religiously diverse country in the world. Canada is also a country of great religious variety.

Fifty years ago, religious diversity in the United States meant Protestants, Catholics, and Jews, but since the 1960s, immigration from Asia, the Middle East, and Africa has dramatically increased the number of people practicing other religions. There are now about six million Muslims, four million Buddhists, and a million Hindus in the United States. To compare these figures to two historically important Protestant denominations in the United States, about 3.5 million are Presbyterians and 2.5 million are Episcopalians. There are more Buddhists in the United States than either of these denominations, and as many Muslims as the two denominations combined. This means that knowing about other religions is not just knowing about people in other parts of the world—but about knowing people in our schools, workplaces, and neighborhoods.

Moreover, religious diversity does not simply exist between religions. It is found within Christianity itself:

• There are many different forms of Christian worship. They range from Quaker silence to contemporary worship with rock music to traditional liturgical worship among Catholics and Episcopalians to Pentecostal enthusiasm and speaking in tongues.

- Christians are divided about the importance of an afterlife. For some, the next life—a paradise beyond death—is their primary motive for being Christian. For other Christians, the afterlife does not matter nearly as much. Instead, a relationship with God that transforms our lives this side of death is the primary motive.
- Christians are divided about the Bible. Some are biblical literalists who believe that the Bible is to be interpreted literally and factually as the inerrant revelation of God, true in every respect and true for all time. Other Christians understand the Bible more symbolically as the witness of two ancient communities—biblical Israel and early Christianity—to their life with God.

Christians are also divided about the role of religion in public life. Some understand "separation of church and state" to mean "separation of religion and politics." Other Christians seek to bring Christian values into public life. Some (commonly called "the Christian Right") are concerned with public policy issues such as abortion, prayer in schools, marriage as only heterosexual, and pornography. Still other Christians name the central public policy issues as American imperialism, war, economic injustice, racism, health care, and so forth. For the first group, values are primarily concerned with individual behavior. For the second group, values are also concerned with group behavior and social systems. The study of religion in North America involves not only becoming aware of other religions but also becoming aware of differences within Christianity itself. Such study can help us to understand people with different convictions and practices.

And there is one more reason why such study is important and exciting: religions deal with the largest questions of life. These questions are intellectual, moral, and personal. Most centrally, they are:

- What is real? The religions of the world agree that "the real" is more than the space-time world of matter and energy.
- How then shall we live?
- How can we be "in touch" with "the real"? How can we connect with it and become more deeply centered in it?

This series will put you in touch with other ways of seeing reality and how to live.

# Chapter 1

# FAITH OF THE FATHERS
## Evangelical History

RELIGION & MODERN CULTURE

Charlotte Street is the saddest section of a declining city. Paint peels off the sides of old houses, and faded sheets serve as makeshift curtains hanging in windows. Poverty, alcoholism, and violent crime are everywhere in this neighborhood. There is, however, a ray of hope. In the midst of the street is a place called Crossroads Community Center. Every Saturday, center volunteers prepare free lunches for everyone who lives in the neighborhood. Young and old alike gather there, creating a rare sense of community solidarity.

In the summer, events take place every weekend at the center—a concert, a magician, clowns, and so on. Each Wednesday, the community center hosts a children's club that provides a chance for kids to do crafts, play games, have Bible lessons, and receive tutoring for their homework. The center also hosts two Alcoholics Anonymous meetings, both filled with recovering alcoholics. Furthermore, the center provides for a variety of practical needs: school supplies for the children at the start of the school year, community cleanup days, gifts for poor families at Christmastime, and so on. Crossroads volunteers try to help each person gain a stronger sense of self-dignity. As they put it, "We want to give a hand up rather than a handout."

The center is not a city service agency, nor is it funded by some big institution. It came about because a group of evangelical Christians from three local churches felt what they call a "burden" for the people of this neighborhood. They are not pushy about religion, but the volunteers say their motivation is "the love of Jesus Christ."

## EVANGELICALS IN NORTH AMERICA TODAY

Evangelicals may be the most influential religious group in North America today. U.S. president George W. Bush speaks about faith in evangelical terms, and evangelicals may have been the key factor in his 2004 reelection. Many evangelicals are involved in helping the poor; large groups of them are also involved in opposing legalized abortion and same-sex marriage, and working for other politically conservative causes. The book *The Purpose Driven Life*, by evangelical pastor Rick Warren, is currently the number-one international best-selling hardback. Also on the best-seller lists are the series of *Left Behind* books by evangelical prophecy teachers Tim LaHaye and Jerry Jenkins. Evangelical activist Jim Wallis's book *God's Politics* is on the best-seller

# GLOSSARY

**benevolent:** Performing good or charitable acts and not seeking to make a profit.

**civil rights:** Rights that all citizens of a society are supposed to have.

**conservative:** Resistant to change when it seeks to replace traditional authority with new ideas.

**liberal:** Open to new ideas; willing to replace tradition with progressive change.

**Pentecost:** The descent of the Holy Spirit upon Christ's followers after his death.

**pentecostal:** Belonging to any Christian denomination that emphasizes the workings of the Holy Spirit, interprets the Bible literally, and adopts an informal and emotional approach to religious worship.

**right-wing:** Belonging to a conservative political group.

**secular:** Not controlled by a religious body or concerned with religious or spiritual matters.

list, too. Black evangelical bishop T. D. Jakes produced a movie, *Woman Thou Art Loosed*, which entered the top-ten box-office sales in 2004. Evangelical pastor Bill Hybels leads a church that attracts more than 17,500 worshipers every week. Furthermore, his Willow Creek Association includes a network of 10,500 churches. In our modern skeptical world, these are amazing statistics.

The word "evangel" is Greek, meaning "good news"—this "good news" is the message that God offers every person the opportunity to enjoy a relationship with him, through his son Jesus Christ. Evangelicals say such a relationship makes one "born again." This new birth enables spiritual growth and service to others. All evangelicals regard the Bible as the inspired word of God, and most believe it is absolute truth.

Evangelicals are Protestant, meaning they belong to the part of Christianity that separated from the Catholic Church in the sixteenth century. They also differ from mainline Protestants, who hold to a less literal understanding of the Bible. Charismatic and pentecostal Christians hold views similar to evangelicals, except they place greater emphasis on the role of the Holy Spirit. Most surveys count charismatics and *pentecostals* as evangelicals.

According to a 2001 survey by the Pew Research Center, 82 percent of U.S. citizens define themselves as Christians. Of those, 23 percent define themselves as white evangelical Protestants, 19 percent as white mainline Protestants, 9 percent as black Protestants, 23 percent as Roman Catholics, and 6 percent as other Christians, including Eastern Orthodox and Mormons.

Evangelicals are less influential in Canada than they are in the United States. In Canada, Catholics outnumber Protestants by about 25 percent. Exact numbers are hard to find, but religious experts agree evangelicals are a minority of Canadian Protestants. The largest Protestant group in the United States is the evangelical Southern Baptist Church, while in Canada the two largest Protestant church groups are the United Church of Canada and the Anglican Church of Canada, both mainstream churches (though a smaller number of Anglican churches also have evangelical beliefs).

*"Suddenly the tears began to flow and I knew without doubt that my sins were forgiven and I was a child of God for all eternity. There wasn't any particular excitement, no sudden surge, just the quiet confidence that I would never have to wonder again about where I would spend eternity. I now had God and he had me."*

*—Oswald Smith, famous Toronto preacher, describes his conversion*

*at a meeting conducted by the evangelist R. A. Torrey*

## PURITAN FOUNDERS

The Puritans planted the first roots of evangelical faith in North America. They arrived in Massachusetts in the seventeenth century, seeking escape from the Church of England, which they regarded as corrupt.

The Puritans believed the Bible was God's blueprint for life. They founded public schools so everyone in their colonies could read scripture. Some historians say colonial Massachusetts was "the best-educated community the world has ever known." Puritan women were literate and often well read, which was unusual at the time. The Puritans founded Ivy League colleges such as Harvard, Princeton, and Yale to train leaders for church and society.

The Puritans sought to order their community life according to Christian ideals, placing common welfare ahead of self-interest. They emphasized that businesses should seek to improve their neighborhoods rather than just make profits. A visitor to a Puritan colony said, "In seven years, I never saw a beggar."

*"With God, I can do all things! But with God and you, and the people who you can interest, by the grace of God, we're gonna cover the world!"*
—Aimee Semple McPherson

## REVIVALS SET COLONIAL AMERICA ON FIRE

Revivals added elements of emotional intensity to Puritan faith. In 1734, Puritan preacher Jonathan Edwards noticed unusual responses to sermons at his Northampton, Massachusetts, church. People sobbed, grew faint, and made earnest commitments to God. Over the next seven years, the same thing happened over all the New England colonies, resulting in more than 50,000 conversions to a new Christian experience.

Shortly after these events, British evangelist George Whitefield came from England to the New England colonies, where he preached to vast crowds in outdoor settings. Before George Washington, Whitefield was the most popular celebrity in North America.

Early in the nineteenth century, a new wave of revivals swept across the frontier regions of the United States. Thousands of people gathered for outdoor "camp meetings," where preachers urged the campers, night and day, to give their lives to Christ. The crowds responded with strong emotions. One observer stated, "No person seemed to wish to go home—hunger and sleep seemed to affect nobody—eternal things were the vast concern."

Revivals added a vital element to evangelical faith. They emphasized that each person must make a personal choice for God. As innumerable evangelicals have proclaimed, "You *must* be born again!" Evangelicals came to define this new birth as a particular point in time where a person made a commitment to enter into a relationship with Christ.

## PREJUDICE & PURITANS

Critic H. L. Mencken once said, "Puritanism is the haunting fear that someone, somewhere, may be happy." Most teens learn about Puritans by reading Nathaniel Hawthorne's classic novel *The Scarlet Letter*. In that novel, the Puritans wear colorless clothes, and are rigid, judgmental, and hypocritical. These portrayals are largely false stereotypes. In fact, Puritans wore colorful and stylish clothes, enjoyed life, and drank beer with meals and rum at weddings. They enjoyed sports—swimming, skating, hunting, fishing, archery, riding, and bowling. However, they did forbid sports on Sundays.

Religious revivals also had lasting social influence. Revival evangelists preached more than personal conversion to Christ; they insisted born-again people must work to improve society. Charles Finney, considered by many to have been the greatest evangelist of the nineteenth century, was adamant that born-again believers could not own slaves. Other revival preachers were also prominent in the movement to end slavery.

## THE BENEVOLENT EMPIRE

Nineteenth-century evangelicals had two goals: personal revival and so-cial reform. By the 1820s, evangelicals had established the "***Benevolent*** Empire," an impressive network of societies committed to bettering the world. Evangelical reformers believed people must be able to read the Bible in order to live happy and successful lives, so they established schools for poor children and illiterate adults. These reformers founded hospitals; nineteenth-century evangelicals began many of today's med-ical centers. In large cities, they established orphanages, soup kitchens, and employment centers. Some evangelicals worked to oppose slavery and warfare while others worked for the rights of women. Oberlin College, founded by revival preacher Charles Finney, was the first U.S. college to admit men and women, black and white, on an equal basis.

## MODERNISTS & FUNDAMENTALISTS DIVIDE

In the late 1800s and early 1900s, North American Protestants divided into two camps. Scientific discoveries and literary ideas caused many Christians to alter their religious beliefs. G. W. F. Hegel redefined God not as a personal being but as a universal "force," and Charles Darwin presented the theory of evolution. Many (but not all) evangelicals felt Darwin's views challenged the Bible's account of creation.

Some Protestants decided they must change their beliefs in light of new discoveries. They doubted the Bible's authority and the existence of miracles. ***Liberal*** preachers gained prominence in large denomina-tions such as the Methodist, Episcopal, and Presbyterian churches that became the mainline churches of today.

At the same time, other clergymen became concerned that these modernist Christians were giving up too much. Critics of the liberal

## THE SCOPES MONKEY TRIAL

In 1925 Dayton, Tennessee, a conspiracy hatched in a local drugstore led to the first public broadcast of a trial and a victory for the antievolutionists.

The state of Tennessee had passed a law making it illegal to teach evolution in schools. In response, the American Civil Liberties Union made an offer to help anyone who was willing to challenge the law. A business owner, school superintendent, and a couple of attorneys talking at a drugstore decided it would be a good way to put their declining town on the map. After all, the teaching of evolution in the schools was one of the major issues of the day.

The drugstore conspirators approached science teacher John Scopes and asked if he had taught evolution. He said yes, and showed where the subject was covered in a state-approved textbook. Scopes agreed to participate in the test case, and the attorneys agreed to prosecute.

William Jennings Bryan was on a national campaign to end the teaching of evolution, and welcomed the opportunity to aid in prosecuting Scopes. Clarence Darrow, an agnostic, jumped at the chance to participate on the defense side. As the trial went on, it became as much about Bryan and Darrow as about Scopes and the law. Darrow even called Bryan as a witness. The drugstore planners had been right—their town grew tremendously thanks to the influx of onlookers and the media.

In what some considered a surprise move, Darrow asked that his client be found guilty so the verdict—and thereby the law—could be appealed to the Tennessee Supreme Court. The jury did so, and Scopes was fined $100. The verdict was later thrown out—on a technicality, not as a ruling on the constitutionality of the antievolution law.

movement decided which Christian beliefs they needed to preserve. They decided that the accuracy of the Bible, deity of Christ, miracles and resurrection of Christ, and belief in his second coming were *fundamental* to Christian faith. Those who insisted on these doctrines called themselves fundamentalists.

In the 1920s, fundamentalists became increasingly angry and isolated from the rest of the world due to social changes that frightened them. In the United States and Canada, skirts became shorter, drinking alcohol gained popularity, and sex was less taboo. In reaction to the "Jazz Age," fundamentalists preached the importance of "separation" from popular culture.

In 1925, the Scopes Monkey Trial broadcast a showdown between fundamentalist William Jennings Bryan and Clarence Darrow, known as "a stern foe of fundamentalists." Though Bryan's client won, Darrow made a laughingstock of Bryan in a trial heard live over the radio by millions of Americans. This trial caused fundamentalists to be even more suspicious of popular culture.

## SPIRITUAL EXPLOSION ON AZUSA STREET

At the beginning of the twentieth century, events took place that would far exceed all previous religious revivals. In 1901, a handful of Bible students in Topeka, Kansas, experienced what they called "speaking in tongues." Similar events took place at a poor urban church on Azusa Street in Los Angeles, California. This event recalled the Bible's description of **Pentecost**, recorded in Acts chapter 2, in which the disciples spoke in unknown languages. Hence, those who spoke in tongues called themselves "pentecostals." The Christians who experienced the "Azusa Street Revival" were black, Latino, and Anglo, so the pentecostal movement spread rapidly across racial lines.

The Azusa Street Revival attracted nationwide attention, and some regard it as the most significant religious event of the past century. Within a decade, huge groups of churches including the Assemblies of God and Church of God had grown from the Azusa Revival.

The pentecostal revival of the early twentieth century caught its second wind in the 1960s with the "charismatic" movement. Worldwide, more than 400 million Christians now claim to be either "pentecostal" or "charismatic." Pentecostal church services typically include lively modern music and joyful, exuberant expressions of faith. In their daily lives, pentecostal and charismatic Christians expect to experience the power of God's Spirit.

# AIMEE SEMPLE MCPHERSON, BILLY GRAHAM, & THE NEW EVANGELICALS

In the 1800s, evangelicals were an important force within the larger picture of U.S. culture. Even those who disagreed with evangelical beliefs respected their charitable works. By the 1920s, however, the evangelical movement had splintered into modernist and fundamentalist camps. Fundamentalists retreated from society, and they lost influence. Events in the 1940s began to reverse that trend. Powerful and innovative Christian leaders led evangelicals away from strict fundamentalism and back to their previous concern for others in society.

Aimee Semple McPherson, born in a farmhouse in Ontario, Canada, in 1890, is a good example of one of these new evangelical leaders. As a teenager, Aimee was skeptical of the Bible, but in 1908, she experienced Christian conversion and spoke in tongues. She married a missionary and traveled with him to China, but he died there of illness. She returned to America a broken young woman. Soon after, however, she received a call from God to preach the Gospel.

"Sister Aimee" was an enormous hit. She was the first woman to drive a car from coast to coast across the United States, and huge crowds flocked to her tent meetings. Settling in Los Angeles in the 1920s, McPherson ordered construction of Angelus Temple, one of the largest churches in America at that time. She started a Christian radio station, and was the first woman to broadcast on a weekly radio show. At Angelus Temple, she presented weekly services that involved jazzy music, staged theater, and props.

Critics and supporters both recognized that Aimee Semple McPherson was doing something new, powerful, and controversial. She was using the methods of popular culture to present evangelical religion. Hollywood had come to the pulpit! In many ways, the large evangelical churches popular throughout North America today have followed the pattern set by Sister Aimee. In her time, Aimee Semple

McPherson was America's best-known Christian speaker. By the time she died in 1944, she had established 410 churches with 29,000 members.

In the 1940s, shortly after the time when Angelus Temple was at its height, a handsome young Baptist preacher began broadcasting his evangelistic sermons over the radio. Billy Graham proclaimed the beliefs of fundamentalists: the Bible was absolute truth, and each person needed to be born again. Unlike his fundamentalist peers, however, Graham was willing to rub shoulders with nonbelievers. As of 2005, in more than sixty-five years of ministry, Graham has preached to over 210 million people in 185 countries. Nearly three million people have responded to his invitations to become "born again."

Billy Graham's fame was an important factor in transforming fundamentalism into a renewed evangelical movement. Another vital factor was the birth of Fuller Theological Seminary. In 1947, Fuller Theological Seminary began training students at its Pasadena, California, campus. For decades, fundamentalists had literally taken the attitude, "to hell with science and *secular* scholarship!" Fuller took a new approach that combined evangelical beliefs with methods of modern scholarship. Fuller still seeks to train men and women to serve as pastors unafraid of the modern world.

## EVANGELICALS SEEK TO EXPAND THEIR INFLUENCE IN MEDIA & POLITICS

In the 1970s and 1980s, evangelicals reached new heights of public influence. *Newsweek* magazine declared 1976 the "year of the evangelical." Although their fundamentalist grandparents had sought to avoid influences of popular culture, some evangelicals in the late twentieth century seemed desirous of controlling the broader culture.

In 1979, Jerry Falwell, a Baptist minister, formed the Moral Majority. Members of the Moral Majority were politically *conservative* evangelicals whose main purpose was to "reverse . . . immorality in our society." The group opposed homosexual rights, abortion, and treaties with the Soviet Union. In 2005, many evangelicals continue to support *right-wing* political causes.

During the 1970s, several evangelical preachers gained fame with their television broadcasts. One of these was Marion G. "Pat" Robertson, who began the Christian Broadcasting Network (CBN). Jim and Tammy Bakker also achieved prominence with their PTL (Praise the Lord) Club television show. The PTL Club eventually ended in scandal, but in its heyday, millions of viewers gained inspiration from the Bakkers and their guests.

In 1986, Pat Robertson announced his candidacy for the Republican presidential nomination. Although he did not win, Robertson brought other evangelicals into political activity. Together with Ralph Reed, Robertson started the Christian Coalition, a group that became a major force in American politics, especially within the Republican Party.

## RELEVANT RELIGION

While some evangelicals were comfortable with the power and influence offered by politics and the media, others were not. Many evangelicals in the late 1970s sought to transform society not by power but by conversion—one soul at a time. Chuck Smith launched the Calvary Chapel Movement in southern California, attracting thousands of surfers and other young people. Also in southern California, John Wimber founded the Vineyard Churches, which combined rock band music during worship services with emphasis on the Holy Spirit's power. He claimed to be "just a fat man going to heaven," but Wimber's movement drew thousands to faith in Christ. In the Midwest, Bill Hybels began the highly successful Willow Creek Church.

In these new churches, drums and guitars replaced organs, and preachers lost their suits and ties. Coffee bars appeared in church hallways, and some churches even built racquetball courts or gyms filled with exercise equipment. Evangelical Christianity in the 1980s was obviously much more "hip" than its ancestor fundamentalism was. The content of evangelical teaching also changed, and most sermons now dealt with practical issues. Messages covered such topics as overcoming addiction, recovering from abuse, healing troubled marriages, relating to teens, and so on.

As the twentieth century has given way to the twenty-first, increasing numbers of evangelicals have been seeking ways to serve others. Evangelical activist Jim Wallis has written a popular book titled *God's Politics* that shows how people of faith can work for social justice, *civil rights*, and peace. Newer evangelical churches establish ministries of service to their communities, alongside programs for their members. Increasingly, evangelicals seek, in the words of Cincinnati Vineyard Pastor Steve Sjogren, "to show God's love in practical ways." Whereas the fundamentalist movement a century ago sought to escape from the world outside their churches, many of today's evangelicals seek ways to serve those in the larger culture.

# Chapter 2

# NEW BIRTH
## Conversion

He was eighteen years old, enjoying the summer between high school and college. His faith had disappeared years ago, because he didn't like to place his confidence in things that were invisible. He had never encountered trouble with the law, but he enjoyed smoking pot and driving cars fast. When a girl he liked invited him to spend a week with a group of her friends at a Young Life camp, he wasn't sure what to say. "Isn't Young Life some kind of born-again Christian thing? Why would I want to do that?"

She explained that yes, it was a born-again Christian thing. However, the camp provided tons of fun activities; it was in a beautiful mountain location, and the only "religious" requirement was to sit through a forty-five-minute daily meeting. That didn't sound so bad, so he went.

The experience literally changed this teen's life. He was amazed by the way volunteer staff members at the camp showed love for the campers; they worked like slaves for a bunch of rowdy, often ungrateful, kids. The brief talks at night made more sense than he expected. After four days, the young man became convinced that God was real and had a plan for his life.

The fifth night, the camp speaker gave all the kids a choice. He said, "We are going to plan no activities for the next hour. We ask you not to speak with another person. We want you to have time to think and to consider life's most important decision. You've heard us talk about Jesus and what he did for you. Go and find a place to be alone. Pray and listen to your heart. If you believe what you've heard this week, then you can ask Jesus to come into your heart. This is your time to decide."

The young man walked to the top of a hill. The night was silent, but a loud debate was going on inside his head. He believed what the speaker had shared that week at camp. At the same time, he was afraid. Accepting Christ would lead him on an entirely new and strange path. Frankly, he enjoyed a number of questionable activities. Was the new life worth giving these up?

Above him, thousands of stars shone in the clear mountain air. He could smell the pines surrounding him. He spoke in a whisper. "God, I've heard everything they said this week. I believe in you. But I'm afraid." He paused, and stared again at the night sky and shadows of the tall trees. "God, I guess if you made all this, you can do a better job running my life than I can. So, I give you my life. I ask Jesus to come into my heart and take control."

He sensed at the time that this exchange was important, but he could

**salvation:** Deliverance from sin or the consequences of sin through Jesus Christ's death on the cross.

not have imagined the extent to which it would alter the entire course of his life. Over the coming months, he quit smoking dope and getting drunk on weekends. He became more polite and thought more of others. While keeping in touch with his old friends, he developed a new set of friends at a Bible study group. He bought a Bible and read it from cover to cover. Some of his companions were pleased with these changes, others were not. All agreed, however, that he had become a different person.

## EVANGELICALS AND THE IMPORTANCE OF A DECISION FOR CHRIST

This young man reached a point where he made a choice about God's role in his life. Not all evangelicals recall such an exact moment of decision. Convictions about Christ may come gradually. One evangelical woman says, "I always tell people that I came to Christ with a big bang and Jim [her husband] came with a slow burn." Evangelicals are less

NEW BIRTH: CONVERSION

*"It's in Christ that we find out who we are and what we are living for. Long before we first heard of Christ, . . . he had his eye on us, had designs on us for glorious living, part of the overall purpose he is working out in everything and everyone."*

*—Ephesians 1:11, from the* Message Bible. *Evangelical pastor Rick Warren quotes this passage on the first page of his best-selling book* The Purpose Driven Life.

concerned with the when or how of conversion than they are with the *who* of conversion.

For evangelicals, it all concerns Jesus Christ. In his best seller *The Purpose Driven Life*, Rick Warren writes, "One day you will stand before God and he will do . . . a final exam, before you enter eternity." Warren explains this "final exam" hinges on a vital question, *"What did you do with my son, Jesus Christ? Did you love him? Did you trust him?"*

For evangelicals, Christ is the solution to humanity's problems. They take seriously the Bible's claim that "All have sinned and fall short of the glory of God" (Romans 3:23). Crime, war, abuse, terrorism, prejudices, addictions, hatred—evangelicals view negative human behaviors as proof that all people share a problem, namely sin. Since God desires a good universe, he must somehow deal with sin. If God allowed evil beings to enter heaven, it would mess up paradise, so something has to change in order for sinners to enjoy God's company.

Evangelicals believe the serious problem of sin required a drastic response—the passion of Jesus Christ. Mel Gibson is a Roman Catholic, yet his movie about Jesus's suffering and death was a huge hit with evangelicals. It graphically portrays the center of evangelical belief,

"while we were yet sinners Christ died for us" (Romans 5:8). As Billy Graham, the most famous evangelical preacher, explains, "No man ever loved like Jesus. He died on the cross to save us. He bore our sins. And now God says, 'Because He did, I can forgive you.'"

Members of other religions find this exclusive focus on Jesus troubling. It seems disrespectful of other traditions. What about Buddha? What about Mohammed? Most evangelicals have no ill feelings toward people of other religions, but they recall Jesus's words, "I am the way and the truth and the life. No one comes to the Father except through me" (John 14:6). Evangelicals feel deep gratitude for Jesus's death on the cross, which they regard as God's unique solution for humanity's needs.

Evangelical scholars disagree regarding the "fine print" of *salvation* through Christ. Some wonder, might there be a second chance to accept Christ after death? Others debate, does hell really exist? If so, is it temporary or eternal? What about those raised in other religious cultures? Some evangelicals, following Christian philosopher C. S. Lewis, suggest that perhaps a Buddhist, Hindu, or anyone else might follow Jesus unknowingly; after all, they reason, Jesus was the love of God made flesh, so people who live lives of love are following Jesus, whether they recognize him or not. Evangelicals vary in their views on these questions, but evangelical leaders agree that they should strive to lead as many people as possible to enjoy a relationship with God through Christ.

## SALVATION IS NEW BIRTH

Evangelicals equate a decision to trust Christ for salvation with the "new birth." Hence, evangelicals and charismatics are born-again believers. The expression, "born again" comes from the third chapter of John's Gospel. Translations of the Greek text differ. Is it "born again" or "born from above"? In either case, the concept is clear—when one receives salvation, her life gets a fresh start.

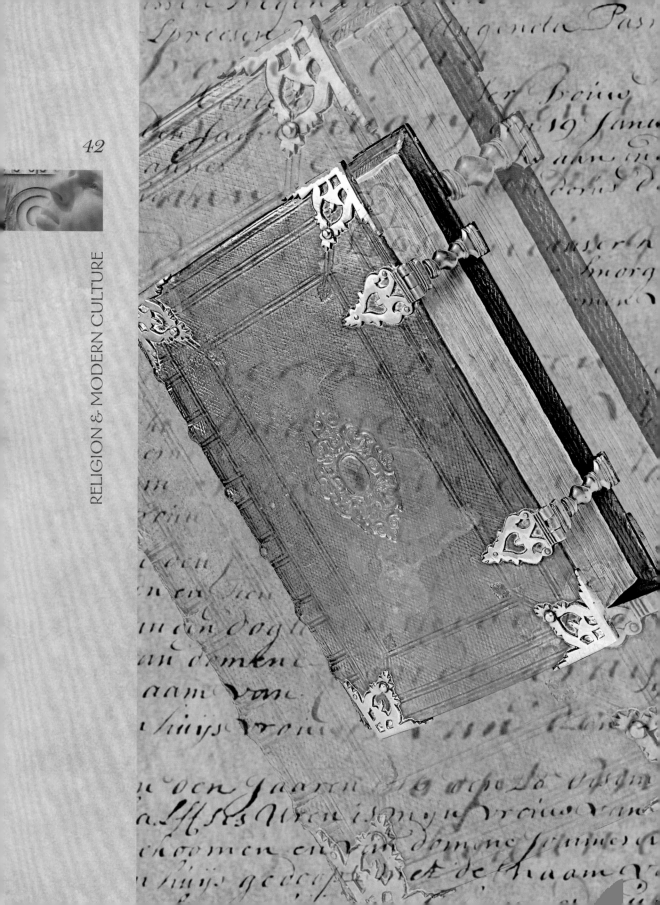

RELIGION & MODERN CULTURE

## FROM KORN TO CHRIST:
## CELEBRITY CONVERSIONS

Early in 2005, Brian "Head" Welch surprised fans of the heavy metal rock band, Korn, when he quit the band. Why? He wished to commit himself wholeheartedly to serving Christ. Welch responded to an "altar call," a time after services at evangelical churches when worshipers come forward to accept Christ as their savior. He had been attending Valley Bible Fellowship in Bakersfield, California, for a few weeks before making the decision. Welch says he was hooked on methamphetamines and could not find a way to kick the habit. He claims that after his conversion, the desire for drugs went away. Welch describes his years with Korn: "I had money, women, drugs of choice," he said. "But none of it brings happiness. You'll never find fulfillment in those things . . . I was so low. I told God, 'Just kill me, please.'" Welch says his decision for Christ made him "the happiest man in the world." A few weeks later, Welch traveled with a group from the church to Israel, where he was baptized (like Christ) in the river Jordan.

Over the years, a number of famous musicians and singers have proclaimed their new birth. Most influential was country music legend Johnny Cash. Others have included Pat Boone, Mark Farner (of Grand Funk Railroad), Charlie Daniels, and Kerry Livgren (Kansas). Folk-rock artist Bob Dylan made a highly publicized profession of Christian rebirth in the 1980s and has puzzled fans regarding his spiritual beliefs for two decades since then.

Of course, evangelicals are not alone in their appreciation for the new birth. Marcus Borg (who believes the Bible contains truth, but not in a literal sense) says, "Being born again . . . is at the very center of the New Testament and the Christian life. We need to reclaim it." At the same time, evangelicals place more emphasis on new birth than other Christians do.

Since Christ paid for all sins on the cross, a reborn believer experiences the gift of forgiveness. She can believe in the Bible promise, "though your sins are as scarlet, they are washed white as snow" (Isaiah 1:18). Psychiatrist Karl Menninger once said that if he could convince his hospital patients someone had forgiven their sins, three-quarters of them could walk out the next day. Evangelicals claim to experience such forgiveness. They view life following conversion as starting over with a "clean slate."

## LIVING THE NEW LIFE

Billy Graham says, "Being a Christian is more than just an instantaneous conversion; it is like a daily process whereby you grow to be more and more like Christ."

A relationship requires time together, so evangelicals urge a daily "quiet time" alone with God. President George W. Bush says this is how he starts his day, and millions of his fellow U.S. citizens would say the same. "Quiet time" involves reading a brief passage from the Bible or a devotional booklet, followed by time spent conversing with God.

Evangelical churches typically offer a broad menu of spiritual-growth classes, and small-group Bible studies are common. Evangelicals gather in homes, in groups of less than a dozen, to read the Bible aloud, discuss its meaning, and pray for one another.

Evangelicals have also produced multimillion-dollar industries to promote spiritual growth. These include radio and television networks,

45

RELIGION & MODERN CULTURE

*"Jesus answered and said to him, 'Most assuredly, I say to you, unless one is born again, he cannot see the kingdom of God.'"*

*—John 3:3*

publishing houses, and recording industries. As of 2005, there were more than 2,000 Christian radio stations in the United States, most of them run by evangelicals. Evangelical book publishers are also doing well. In 2005, Tyndale House Publishers announced a plan to purchase fifty-six acres for warehouses to store their books; they also reported making $122 million in annual profits. A few believers are uncomfortable with the size and scope of Christian industries, wondering if perhaps Jesus's anger at moneymakers in the Temple might say something to today's multimillion-dollar Christian corporations. However, for the most part, evangelicals are pleased to enjoy a superabundance of products that promote spiritual growth.

Even with the biggest assortment of Christian books, CDs, and DVDs on the planet, few North American evangelicals claim the Christian life is easy. Billy Graham says, "The Christian life is not a constant high. I have my moments of deep discouragement. I have to go to God in prayer with tears in my eyes, and say, 'O God, forgive me,' or 'Help me.'" For millions of evangelicals, the new life includes struggles—and yet it remains satisfying.

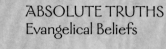

# Chapter 3

# ABSOLUTE TRUTHS
## Evangelical Beliefs

Lee Strobel recalls the time in his life when he lost faith in God—and the point at which he refound it. He always has had a critical mind, and as a high school freshman, when he learned the beginning of life could come about through chemical processes, Strobel reasoned that made God unnecessary. "And so," he says, "when I saw the evidence that God was unnecessary, I jettisoned God."

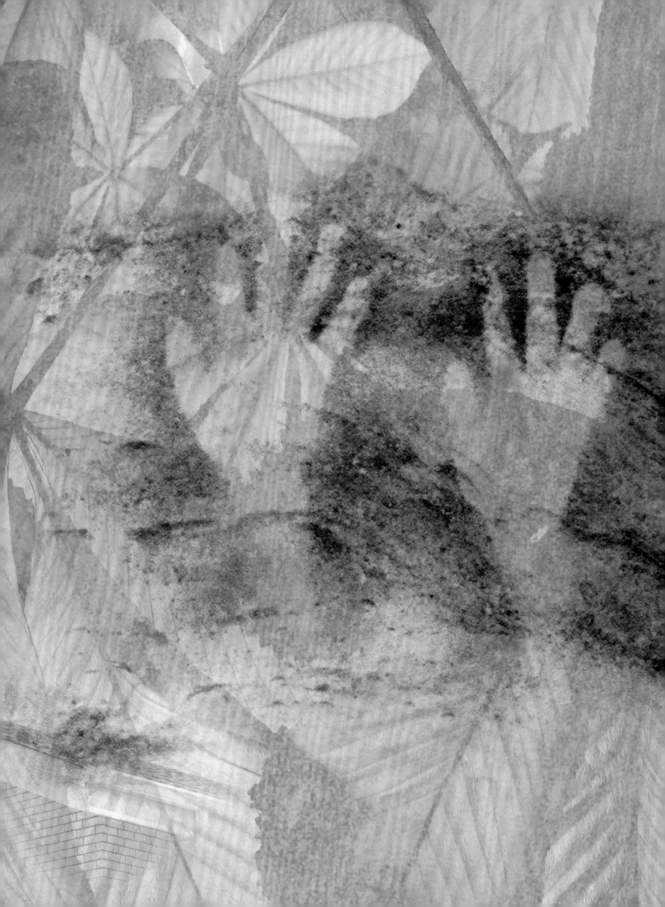

Strobel went on to serve as legal editor for the *Chicago Tribune*. His work covering legal cases reminded him of how important even the tiniest piece of evidence could be. When his wife became an evangelical Christian, Strobel decided to go over the Gospel records of Christ's life as if they were a legal case. Was there solid evidence for Jesus's life and deeds? Strobel applied his legal and journalistic training to an in-depth investigation of that question. In his book *The Case for Christ*, Strobel records his conclusions:

> After a personal investigation that spanned more than six hundred days and countless hours, my own verdict is the case for Christ was clear. . . . As someone educated in journalism and law, I was trained to respond to the facts, wherever they lead. For me, the data demonstrated convincingly that Jesus is the Son of God.

After leaving his job with the *Tribune*, Strobel became teaching pastor for Willow Creek Church (Bill Hybel's enormous congregation in Illinois). From there, he went on to his current job as anchor for the PAX television show *Faith Under Fire*. He has also written a number of books including *The Case for Christ*, *The Case for Faith*, and *The Case for a Creator*.

Lee Strobel is a good representative for evangelical beliefs, since most evangelicals are insistent that their faith depends on *proof*. Their fundamentalist ancestors despised science and scholarship, and many lost influence as a result. When the new evangelicals came out of fundamentalism in the 1940s, they were determined not to repeat those mistakes. Therefore, today's evangelical thinkers try hard to show their beliefs are compatible with physics, archaeology, philosophy, and history.

Like many other evangelicals, Strobel is adamant that the Bible is accurate and truthful. While they have left behind the anger and rigidity of fundamentalism, most of today's evangelicals also avoid the liberal (or modernist) extremes that fundamentalists opposed. The majority of evangelicals are still passionate in their attachments to the "fundamentals" of belief as defined by their ancestors. These include the literal truth of the Bible, actual miracles in the Bible, and the deity and resurrection of Jesus Christ.

## CERTAIN OF THE BASICS—
## BUT DIVIDED REGARDING DETAILS

Evangelicals are adamant that their beliefs are "absolute truths," yet they disagree with one another regarding the details of those truths. Unlike Catholics, evangelicals lack a single spokesperson for their faith. Unlike mainline Protestant groups, they rarely have bishops or large governing bodies. Therefore, they lack a means to enforce common thinking. Evangelicals have always insisted they get truth from "the Bible alone," yet they differ as to what the Bible says.

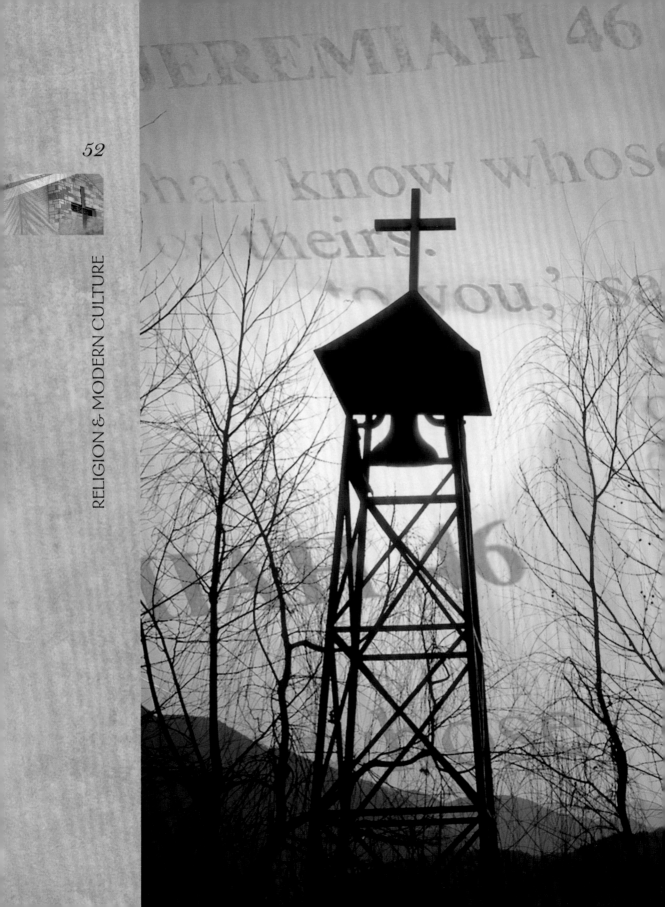

RELIGION & MODERN CULTURE

*"All Scripture is Godbreathed and is useful for teaching, rebuking, correcting and training in righteousness, so that the man of God may be thoroughly equipped for every good work."*

—2 Timothy 3:16

For instance, Evangelicals differ regarding the lasting effects of salvation: is it "once saved always saved" or can one walk away from Christ? They differ in their beliefs regarding destiny: is it all predestined or is it up to our free will? Related to that issue, they are divided about the limits of God's knowledge: does God "see" the future or just the past? They have varying views about baptism: should babies or adult believers be baptized?

The diversity of evangelical beliefs is evident in their major schools. Regent College in Vancouver, Canada; Fuller Theological Seminary in Pasadena, California; Gordon-Conwell Seminary in South Hamilton, Massachusetts; and Trinity Evangelical Divinity School in Deerfield, Illinois: each employ professors with a varied set of beliefs. These evangelical schools require agreement on certain basics, yet they encourage diversity in the details of faith. Learning a variety of views, students are better prepared to make choices regarding personal faith.

While some other Christians criticize this broad diversity of opinions, it has helped evangelicals more than it has hindered them. The evangelical movement is a "big tent," able to hold many beliefs and personalities. Evangelicals often work together despite theological differences —thus increasing their public influence.

## INFALLIBLE SCRIPTURE

Name-callers have at times referred to evangelicals as "Bible thumpers." In return, one evangelical Christian rock song from the 1970s declared,

"Well they call me a Bible thumper—and I do believe it's true. If they only knew what was in the Word of God, they'd be out thumpin' that Bible too!"

Evangelicals are proud to inherit a tradition started five hundred years ago by Martin Luther. The German monk defied the pope, risked death, and permanently divided Christianity because he believed the Bible alone should be the standard for Christian truth. They also agree with John Wesley, the founder of Methodism in the eighteenth century, who said the Bible is, "a most solid and precious system of divine truth, wherein is no defect, no excess. It is the fountain of heavenly wisdom."

Evangelical sermons, books, even music videos all claim to derive authority from the Bible. The Bible is absolute truth for evangelicals; however, it is not cold truth. Evangelicals liken the Bible to "a love letter from God." When she reads a certain passage in the morning, an evangelical believer may consider that passage to be "God's message to me for today."

Though evangelicals agree the Bible is truth, they sometimes differ regarding the limitations of that statement. Some believe the Bible speaks with authority regarding moral, practical, and religious truths— and regarding science and history. Thus, for example, the first chapters of Genesis must be literally true descriptions of earth science. Others would agree that the Bible is literally true regarding "faith and practice," but not necessarily so regarding scientific issues. As one theologian put it, "The Bible tells us how to go to heaven, but not how the heavens go."

## ANSWERED PRAYER

Twenty-five years ago, the Brooklyn Tabernacle Church in New York City had less than two dozen members. Today, it has more than six thousand. The growth, according to Pastor Jim Cymbala, is due to prayer. In his popular book *Fresh Wind, Fresh Fire*, Pastor Cymbala says, "I have seen God do more in people's lives in ten minutes of real prayer

## A TURNING POINT IN THE LIFE OF AMERICA'S MOST FAMOUS PREACHER

In *The Purpose Driven Life*, Rick Warren relates an anecdote concerning Billy Graham: "In the early years of his ministry, Billy Graham went through a time when he struggled with doubts about the accuracy and authority of the Bible. One moonlit night he dropped to his knees in tears and told God that, in spite of confusing passages he didn't understand, from that point on he would completely trust the Bible." Warren concludes, "From that day forward, Billy's life was blessed with unusual power and effectiveness."

than in ten of my sermons." Cymbala insists, "God is not aloof. He says continuously through the centuries, 'I'll help you. I really will. When you're ready to throw up your hands, throw them up to me.'"

Prayer is important for many North Americans. A December 2004 survey by *U.S. News & World Report* found that 64 percent of U.S. citizens pray more than once a day. The 2003 Ipsos-Reid survey of religion in Canada found that 45 percent of Canadian citizens pray daily. Evangelicals place special emphasis on prayer. In Barna surveys, more than 80 percent of respondents who claim to be "born again" pray daily. More than other religious groups, evangelicals are likely to focus on "intercessory" prayer; in other words, they pray and ask God to do things.

55

RELIGION & MODERN CULTURE

*"You will receive power when the Holy Spirit falls on you."*

—*words of Jesus in Acts 1:8*

Innumerable evangelical books, seminars, sermons, and videos emphasize the power of God to answer prayer.

Evangelicals agree that prayer changes things, but they find it difficult to explain the mechanism by which that happens. Most evangelical scholars believe God exists outside of time and thus has already experienced the future. One writer compares God to a person reading a book. Mortals are stuck on a certain page partway through the book; we cannot see the pages ahead of our time. God, however, can pick up the book of history at any point—he can read pages that are still "future" from our perspective.

This belief raises a question: If God already knows the future, why bother asking him for things? What difference can prayer make? Christians who believe in God's knowledge of the future answer that God knows what will happen, yet he nonetheless enjoys hearing prayers and responding to his children's cries. Not all evangelicals agree with this view.

Gregory Boyd, professor of theology at Bethel College, promotes what he calls the "open view" of God. In this view, God knows everything that now takes place in the world. However, God does not yet know the future—he cannot. Out of love for his creatures, he has given them the freedom to choose—to act or not to act, to love or not to love. Thus, each prayer is actually "news" to God. Those who support the open view of God say prayer is especially vital in their understanding, because what will happen in the future depends in large part on whether people pray.

# THE POWER OF THE HOLY SPIRIT

In 1958, Pastor David Wilkerson felt drawn to members of youth gangs in New York City. Wilkerson led Nicky Cruz, a young Puerto Rican gang member, to begin a new life with Christ. Nicky Cruz then met a heroin addict named Sonny Arguinzoni. He told Arguinzoni, "If God could free me from gang life, he can free you from addiction." As Arguinzoni remembers: "Before you knew it, I'd raised my hands and was saying, 'Thank you Lord, Thank you Jesus.' I kept saying it over and over . . . and suddenly I was singing and shouting and it wasn't in English, but in some strange language that kept flowing off my tongue." Sonny Arguinzoni had received the baptism of the Holy Spirit.

Shortly after that, Arguinzoni purchased a house in the Boyle Heights section of Los Angeles, where there was much crime. Gang members, prostitutes, and addicts found refuge there, and a surprising number turned their lives around. This was the beginning of Victory Outreach. Today, Victory Outreach is a major pentecostal denomination with over 200,000 members in more than 500 churches. The Victory Outreach Web site declares:

> We have grown into one of the largest inner city ministries and pentecostal denominations in the world, meeting the needs of people from all walks of life. For 37 years, Victory Outreach has trained and equipped men and women to reach their full potential in life, whether it is establishing a church, building a business, or growing and nurturing a family.

Most Christians believe in the Holy Spirit who is a part of the Holy Trinity (one of the three forms of God in Christian belief). However,

pentecostals and charismatics place more emphasis on the real and practical power of the Holy Spirit than do other Christians. This belief in the Spirit's power has enabled pentecostals and charismatics to achieve remarkable success in evangelism. Worldwide, there are more than 11,000 charismatic and pentecostal churches, and there are more than 20 million pentecostals in the United States and perhaps as many as 400 million worldwide. No religious movement in history compares with the growth of pentecostals and charismatics.

Pentecostals and charismatics emphasize a spiritual experience they call "Baptism with the Holy Spirit," which is a separate event from Christian conversion. Pentecostals regard this as a "second step" in Christian growth, coming after new birth. Baptism of the Spirit involves speaking in tongues, transmitted by the laying on of hands. Sonny Arguinzoni gives a good description of this experience: "suddenly I was singing and shouting and it wasn't in English, but in some strange language that kept flowing off my tongue." Pentecostals believe all Christians can and should have this experience; charismatics are less definite on that point. Pentecostals and charismatics claim the Baptism of the Holy Spirit enables believers to become more like Jesus than they would have been without this experience.

## CREATION

If you ever drive toward Los Angeles from Palm Springs, California, you will pass an amazing site on highway 10. Just off the freeway, Cabazon, California, is home to the world's two largest dinosaurs. "Dinny" the Apatosaurus and "Rex" the Tyrannosaurus are enormous concrete sculptures. If you pull off the freeway, you can actually go inside Dinny's tummy, which is big enough to house a combination museum and gift shop. If that is not astonishing enough, Dinny and Rex are gargantuan dinosaurs with a message. As you head toward the doorway located in the Apatosaurus' tail, a sign reads "From *primordial* soup, to the zoo, to you, is evolution true?" According to the dinosaurs' owners, evolution is a falsehood. They believe dinosaurs and humans appeared at approximately the same time, in recent history. The Cabazon dinosaurs are a "creation mission" intended to promote so-called "creation science."

For more than a century, scientists and religious scholars have been puzzling over human origins. In the minds of most scientists, fossil remains and genetic research prove life on earth evolved over millions of years. The beginning of the Bible says God created life over six days. This presents little problem for Christians who regard the Bible more symbolically, but it forms a challenge for Bible literalists. How can the Bible and science be reconciled?

Many evangelicals reject the findings of science regarding evolution. Doing so, they are following the traditions of the earlier fundamentalist movement. The Creation Research Society and the Institute for Creation Research attempt to prove their particular interpretation of the Bible by means of their own allegedly scientific study, replacing secular science with their own. Creation science claims all modern forms of scientific dating are flawed and alleges the world is only thousands of years old, rather than millions. According to this view, Noah's flood caused the extinction of dinosaurs, along with the creation of fossils and the Grand Canyon. Many evangelical children enjoy books and tapes produced by the *creationists*, because they show people living alongside dinosaurs during Bible times. Secular scientists are unimpressed.

Other evangelicals see no conflict between the accounts of creation in science and in Genesis. Hugh Ross, a scientist and founder of an evangelical organization called Reasons to Believe, says the "days" of creation in Genesis are long periods of time. Reading the Bible this way, Ross says the scientific theory of evolution corresponds amazingly well with the Bible account of creation, where life proceeds from the seas to the land, from simple to more complicated. Another set of evangelical

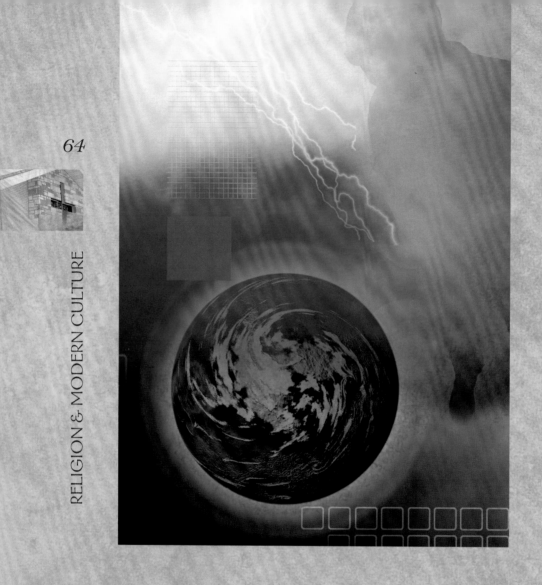

scholars regards the opening chapters of Genesis as theological—rather than scientific—truth. They believe the account in Genesis is more like a painting than a photograph of what happened in the beginning; its details are true, but they are metaphor and poetry, not science. According to these scholars, the focus of Genesis is on the fact that God is responsible for creation, apart from any concern with the exact method of creation.

## THE END TIMES

Evangelicals are believers in God's role at the beginning of the world—and at the end. The series of *Left Behind* novels, written by evangelical authors Tim LaHaye and Jerry B. Jenkins, have sold over 62 million copies and inspired a movie and television series. These books present the authors' interpretations of the Bible's book of Revelation and end-time events. According to an article in *Newsweek*, one in eight Americans has read a book in the *Left Behind* series. Critics don't like the way the books are written; nonetheless, Tim LaHaye and Jerry Jenkins are America's best-selling fiction authors. They have inspired millions with their interpretations of Bible prophecy, and they claim more than three thousand people have become Christians because of their books. Many readers of the *Left Behind* novels believe Jesus is likely to return soon.

The book of Revelation has long puzzled interpreters. Many Bible scholars, including some evangelicals, interpret the book symbolically. Others, such as LaHaye and Jenkins, interpret Revelation more literally. All evangelicals share a belief in Jesus's second coming, yet many are unconcerned with the details. More than a few preachers have pointed out that God is going to do what he has planned regardless of human theories. Evangelicals hold a broad diversity of beliefs regarding the end times. (For in-depth information about the book of Revelation, end-time prophecies, and evangelical beliefs regarding them, read the Mason Crest book *Prophecies and End-Time Speculations: The Shape of Things to Come*.)

*Chapter 4*

## FAMOUS EVANGELICALS

RELIGION & MODERN CULTURE

In 2005, at age eighty-three, Billy Graham was still a noble, powerful figure with deep-set eyes and a magnetic voice. People around the world recognized his name.

As a boy, Billy enjoyed baseball and Tarzan comic books. One of his teachers declared in class that he would probably never amount to much. At the age of sixteen, Billy went to a revival meeting and became a Christian. He married Ruth Bell in 1943, and in 1947, he began to hold crusades in large tents around the country and later, around the world. Thousands attended. Every night he invited the audience to come forward to accept Jesus Christ into their lives; many accepted his invitation.

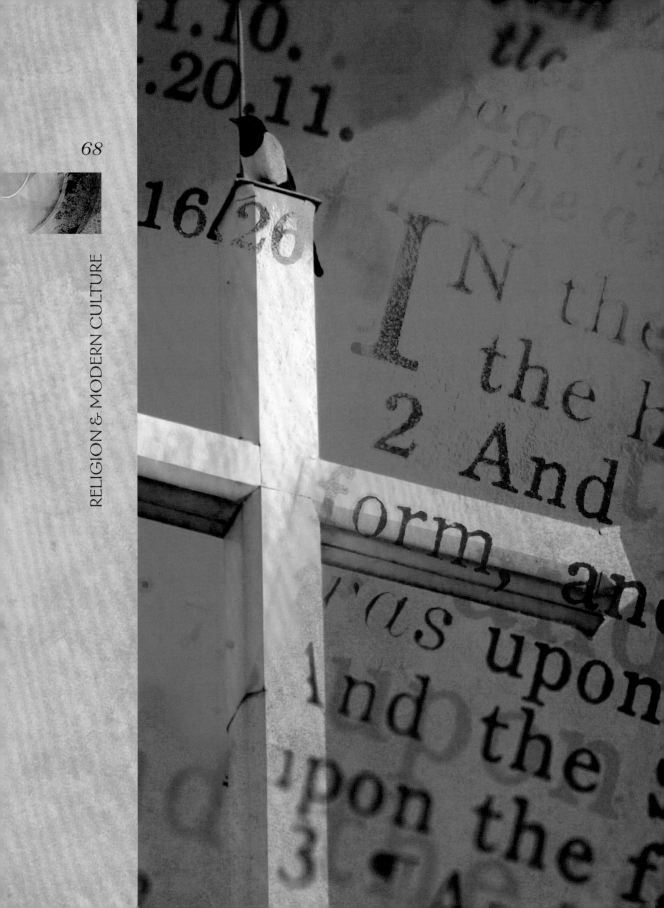

RELIGION & MODERN CULTURE

> *"The History of the world is but the biography of great men."*
>
> —*Thomas Carlyle*

These crusades continued for nearly sixty years. Billy has authored several books and has had a long television and radio ministry. The Grahams have five grown children and many grandchildren.

Ruth Bell, born to medical missionary parents to China, developed a love for God at an early age. Ruth has had a major part in raising their five children, designed their family home in Montreat, North Carolina, and was an active part in Billy Graham's ministry. She also played an important role in the Ruth and Billy Graham Children's Health Center Foundation.

Gigi Graham, the eldest of the Graham children, married clinical psychologist Dr. Stephan Tchividjian. They live in Florida and have seven children and eleven grandchildren. She is a successful writer and a speaker at women's conferences and conventions across the United States.

Anne Graham, the second of the Graham children, married Dan Lotz and has three grown children. She is a gifted Bible teacher, an award-winning author, and is on the board of the Billy Graham Association.

Ruth Graham is the youngest of the daughters. She is married to Richard McIntyre. They have four children and one grandchild. She has struggled with people's expectations of her because of being a Graham, especially when her first marriage at age eighteen ended in divorce, but she has used this experience to help others through her speaking engagements and writings.

Franklin Graham is the older of the two Graham boys. In his late teens, he rebelled, but on a trip to the Holy Land with a friend, he decided to "straighten out his life." He and his wife, Jane, have four children and one grandchild. He founded World Medical Missions, Inc. and Samaritan's Purse, was ordained as a minister in 1981, and took charge of his father's ministry in 1996.

Ned Graham, the Grahams' youngest child, also had a rebellious adolescent and college life. He and his wife, Carol, have two sons and live in China. Ned is president of East Gates Ministries, a small mission to help Christians in China.

Clearly, Graham, his wife, and their children have all been important influences in the evangelical movement and beyond.

## RICK WARREN

Have you ever asked yourself "What am I doing here?" Rick Warren answers this question in his book *The Purpose Driven Life*. It is the best-selling hardback nonfiction book in history. Its theme is that people find meaning in life by following God's purposes. Millions of people have participated in 40 Days of Purpose reading groups.

Rick is the very successful pastor of Saddleback Church in Lake Forest, California. When Rick and his wife moved to the Saddleback Valley, their dream was to start a church for the depressed, the hurting, and the confused—a church where people could find love, acceptance, and hope. Today, twenty years later, the church has an attendance of some 22,000 each weekend. Rick has a plan for Saddleback's network of 40,000 churches to tackle issues such as disease, poverty, and ignorance.

*Time* and *Christianity Today* have named Rick Warren "the most influential pastor in America." Rick is also the author of *The Purpose Driven Church*, winning the Gold Medal Medallion Award. Tens of thousands of churches have followed its model of church growth. Rick lives with his wife, Kay, and their three children in Trabuco Canyon, California. Some believe Warren is the successor of Billy Graham for the role of America's minister.

## MITIGATING A HOSTAGE CRISIS

In March of 2005, *The Purpose Driven Life* played a curious role in a hostage situation. Brian Nichols, accused of three murders, held twenty-six-year-old Ashley Smith at gunpoint in her Atlanta apartment. Smith, the mother of a five-year-old daughter, had seen her husband murdered four years before this incident. Smith asked the man if she could read to him, and did so from the Bible and *The Purpose Driven Life*. She told her captor that God had a plan for his life, perhaps to go to prison and share faith with the prisoners there. After she cooked him some pancakes, the criminal allowed Smith to leave to get her daughter. Shortly afterward, police surrounded the apartment, and he gave himself up to them. This incident caused Ashley Smith to become an instant celebrity, boosted sales of Rick Warren's book, and demonstrated how loving one's enemy can transform a horrible situation into a hopeful one.

## JAMES DOBSON AND FOCUS ON THE FAMILY

Dr. James C. Dobson is best known for his daily radio program *Focus on the Family*, which is heard on 8,300 radio stations, in twenty-five languages, and in 164 countries. The program helps families with issues of

childrearing, family health, and faith. Dr. Dobson also has a daily TV show on eighty stations across the United States. He is the author of at least twenty books on family issues, has made four film series, and has won numerous awards and recognitions.

Dr. Dobson earned a Ph.D. from the University of Southern California in the field of child development and is listed in *Who's Who in Medicine and Health Care.* He headed the U.S. national campaign against same-sex marriage in 2003 and 2004. Political analysts say that by using his influence over white evangelicals, Dobson helped President Bush win the swing states of Florida and Ohio in the 2004 presidential election. Dr. Dobson has been very involved in family-related government activities. He, his wife Shirley, and their two grown children live in Colorado.

## JIM WALLIS

Jim Wallis is one of the most important Christian leaders on issues of social justice and poverty. Over thirty years ago, he started Sojourners, a nationwide network of Christians for peace and justice. He is still the editor in chief of their magazine. Jim is an activist, international commentator, speaker, author, columnist, and preacher. He helped form Call to Renewal, a Christian organization working to overcome poverty. Numerous newspapers across the United States have published Wallis's columns. He has taught at Harvard University on "Faith, Politics and Society" and speaks at more than two hundred events a year. Wallis is the author of seven books. His newest one is *God's Politics: Why the Right Gets It Wrong and the Left Doesn't Get It* (2005).

Jim was inspired as a teenager to branch out of his white, segregated church. He got to know the black neighborhoods and churches of inner-city Detroit. While at Trinity Evangelical Divinity School in Illinois, one of his friends cut out the thousands of verses in the Bible that talk

*"My primary concern is that all of us—Democrats, Republicans, everyone—are getting religion about the things that are closest to the heart of God, things like a silent tsunami that has taken the lives of 30,000 children each and every day from hunger and diseases related to hunger. I often ask people, 'What do you think God is most preoccupied with, those 30,000 children dying every day or whether we call it civil unions or gay civil marriage? Which do you think God spends the most time worrying about?'"*

—*Jim Wallis, in an interview with David Ian Miller on SF Gate.com, regarding his book* God's Politics.

about the poor. When finished, his Bible was truly a holy book—it was full of holes. Jim took this Bible when he preached in order to help Christians see the importance God places on issues of poverty.

Jim and his wife, Joy, have two sons, Luke and Jack. In an interview on *30 Good Minutes*, a TV program on WTTW in Chicago, Wallis shared that in neighborhoods like his—full of drugs, despair, and danger—the only way to break the cycle is through hope. "But without hope, there isn't a social program in the world that'll change poverty in my neighborhood, fourteen blocks from the White House, where the kids go to bed with the sound of gunfire at night." What Wallis calls "my best line" is a paraphrase of a verse in Hebrews, "hope is believing in spite of the evidence and watching the evidence change."

## A LIFE LESSON AT THE SPECIAL OLYMPICS

John Mark Ministries' Web site tells a story adapted from the Joni and Friends Web site. Several years ago Ken Tada was officiating at a Special Olympics event. During one of the races, a participant left the track and started running toward his friends in the infield. Another participant, a girl with Down syndrome, stopped short of the finish line, calling, "Stop, come back, this is the way." Seeing the other runner was confused, she ran to him, wrapped his arm in hers, and ran with him to finish last in the race. The other competitors hugged them, and the spectators gave them a standing ovation. The girl taught the observers a lesson that day: "it's important to take time out from our own goals in life to help others find their way."

## JOYCE MEYER

Joyce Meyer teaches that no matter what a person's background or mistakes, God has a place for her and can help her enjoy life. She speaks from experience. Born in 1943, Joyce had a turbulent childhood. She was sexually molested. Married at age eighteen, she divorced shortly thereafter. Joyce then married David B. Meyer. Still not happy, Joyce cried

out to God, an action she says helped her get a hold on life. Joyce and David have now been married for more than thirty-five years and have four children.

Joyce spent five years as associate pastor and then established her own pentecostal Christian ministry. Joyce Meyer Ministries is dedicated to helping people know the Bible. She believes if Christians truly understand the Bible, they can learn to live successfully, and help others do the same.

Reverend Meyer has a mainly female audience. Her television program broadcasts to two-thirds of the globe, her radio program is carried on four hundred radio stations, and she has authored seventy books. A Christian watchdog group has asked the IRS to look into the finances of Joyce's ministries. A representative for her group says 93 percent of their monthly income goes to more than 150 worldwide charities, so they are not worried about an investigation.

## AMY GRANT

Amy Grant is one of Christian music's most significant performers. She grew up in Nashville, Tennessee, and her first album was released when Amy was just sixteen. In 1982, she married singer-songwriter Gary Chapman.

The 1980s were an exciting time for Amy. She became a gospel star, won numerous Grammy and Dove awards, had certified platinum and gold albums, and won a nomination for artist of the year. She also made it to number one on the pop charts with her duet with Peter Cetera, "The Next Time I Fall in Love." In the late 1980s and early 1990s, Amy became a secular pop star. This brought criticism from the evangelical world, but Amy didn't let this deter her. Soon she became popular in both secular and Christian circles.

Amy Grant's success continued in the 1990s with three hit singles. Her album *Every Heartbeat* sold five million copies. In 1999, Amy and Gary divorced, and the evangelical community reacted with scorn. Grant eventually married longtime collaborator Vince Gill. Amy says of her music, "The point of my songs is never singer focused. It's experience focused. When I go into the studio, I'm taking my experience as a wife and a mother with me."

## JONI EARECKSON TADA

When she was a teenage girl, a diving accident left Joni Eareckson a quadriplegic. Joni learned how to paint with her teeth during the first two years after her accident, and she produces beautifully detailed art. Her name became famous in countries around the world due to her biography and a film about her life, titled *Joni.*

Joni started Joni and Friends, a ministry to other people with disabilities. Over a million listeners a week hear her daily five-minute radio program with that same name. Retreats put on by Joni and Friends provide inspiration and relaxation for families with disabled children. Wheels for the World, one of Joni's organizations, has collected 25,000 used wheelchairs from across the United States. Inmates in prisons refurbish these and send them to disabled people around the world.

Joni's accomplishments, awards, and honorary degrees are amazing. A person with full movement would have a difficult time keeping up with her. She is the author of over thirty books. Joni and Ken Tada have been married since 1982, when she became Joni Eareckson Tada.

## T. D. JAKES

When he was a youngster, T. D. Jakes, now also known as Bishop Thomas Dexter Jakes, attended meetings where his mother spoke. The boy told his mother that someday she would be attending meetings where he spoke. He was right.

Jakes came from a hard-working family. Although he dropped out of high school to help care for his sick father and later his mother, Jakes eventually got his GED and also finished college.

Today, Jakes dynamically addresses people's deep-felt needs. Many see him as a man who understands their inner beings. He speaks to the abuse, emotional or physical, that people have experienced and helps them get past their pain to live in hope. One of his most famous sermons is "Woman Thou Art Loosed," full of healing and inspiration for today's women. An R-rated movie about sexual abuse, based on the book, was a box-office top-ten film. Jakes has written several best-selling books, and he pastors the Potter's House in Dallas, a nondenominational, multiracial church of 35,000 people that reaches out to the poor in many ways.

## J. I. PACKER

The 340,000 readers of *Christianity Today* magazine named James Innell Packer as the second most influential Christian of the twentieth century. He was born in England, and as a child, he was restricted in physical activities due to an automobile accident. James had a difficult childhood, in part because of this. After reading C. S. Lewis and the Bible while attending Oxford University, he committed his life to following Jesus Christ. In 1979, after teaching and preaching in England for twenty-seven years, he became a professor at Regent College in Canada. He serves as senior editor of *Christianity Today* and enjoys tapping his foot to classic jazz.

Packer has authored over forty books. His book *Knowing God* has inspired Christians to come to know God in a more personal and intimate way and has increased unity between Christian groups.

## BILL HYBELS

Bill Hybels is the founder of Willow Creek Community Church in the Chicago suburb of South Barrington. When the church started in 1975, Christians might have voted it least likely to succeed. It began in an old

movie theater, as a spin-off from a youth group. Today, it is probably the most watched and imitated Christian church in the United States.

In 2005, Bill Hybels, at the age of fifty-two, leads a network of 10,500 churches and gives training to 100,000 pastors a year. When he began his congregation thirty years ago, his goal was to reach out to "seekers" of the Christian faith. At the core of the church's philosophy is the desire for cultural relevancy, excellence, and community. The church consists of many small groups in which members participate. It has live bands, simple sermons, free child care, short services, and approximately 20,000 members in attendance at its four weekend services.

These evangelical leaders differ in many ways. They are black, white, and Hispanic; male and female; young and old; politically liberal and politically conservative. But they all agree on one thing: when Christians reach out to those around them, Jesus Christ has the power to change the world.

# Chapter 5

# GROWING UP
# EVANGELICAL

RELIGION & MODERN CULTURE

On April 20, 1999, Columbine High School in Colorado made headlines across North America when two teenagers opened fire on schoolmates, killing and wounding many, and then killing themselves. Cassie Bernall was a seventeen-year-old student doing research in the library that morning. When one of the gunmen asked her if she believed in God, she responded, "Yes," and he shot her.

*"It takes tremendous courage to say yes to God in the face of death; it takes courage of another kind to keep saying yes to God while living every day in an incredulous and jaded culture."*

—*Wendy Murray Zoba, associate editor, reflecting on Cassie Bernall,* Christianity Today, *November 1, 1999.*

In the book, *She Said Yes*, her mother, Misty Bernall, tells of the struggle she and her husband had to raise children in the evangelical faith. Peer pressure and adolescent troubles caused Cassie to stray from Christianity for a time. The Bernalls were persistent in guiding and setting boundaries for Cassie, and at some point before that fateful morning in April, Cassie rededicated herself to God.

Evangelical parents hope to see their children grow up in the Christian faith. This is difficult in a culture that in many ways is contrary to Christian values. **Materialism** and different sexual standards are some of the conflicts. From taking children to church beginning in infancy, to sending them to Christian schools and colleges, evangelical parents try to influence their offspring to keep the faith.

## SCHOOLS: HOME SCHOOL, PRIVATE, OR PUBLIC?

Like most parents, evangelicals feel a responsibility to educate their children in the best manner possible. At the same time, they are concerned that their sons and daughters be educated with a Christian worldview. Some choose to let their children go through public schools, others prefer Christian schools, and some decide to home school their children.

# GLOSSARY

**materialism:** A way of looking at life that places value on material things (objects that can be seen and touched) rather than on spiritual or moral values.

According to those who advocate home schooling, when a child is educated at home, parents can integrate a Christian point of view into every area of learning. Furthermore, students can learn at their own pace and with their own learning style. Approximately 1,230,000 children in the United States are home schooled. In Canada, home schooling is called home-based learning, and according to some estimates, over 80,000 students get their education in this way. Critics of home schooling say those students who learn at home do not experience the diversity of modern culture and may be unexposed to the ideas and beliefs of their fellow citizens.

Christian private schools are another favorite choice of evangelical parents. These schools provide reinforcement for what children learn about God at home and church. Evangelicals have founded and staffed many Christian schools. The quality of private evangelical schools varies considerably: some have a higher educational standard than the

RELIGION & MODERN CULTURE

## COULD YOU KISS DATING GOODBYE?

Sex and dating are two issues that concern evangelical parents. In the controversial book *I Kissed Dating Goodbye*, author Joshua Harris encourages Christian young people to evaluate our dating culture. It is not so much a book against dating as a book encouraging single people to love with what Harris calls "smart love." Smart love concentrates on loving God and others before one's self, whereas the primary thought when dating is often, "What can I get out of this?" Harris believes our dating culture has many flaws: it brings intimacy but not commitment, it tends to skip the friendship stage, and it makes a physical relationship seem like love. He says dating isolates a couple from important relationships, distracts a person from preparing for the future, and often does not let someone see the true character of another person. Harris writes that God gives us singleness as a gift, for a time. In his opinion, there is no magic formula for finding the right life partner, but there are principles for relationships. They should start out as a casual friendship, go into deeper friendship, then go into intimacy with integrity (morality and honesty), and then engagement. He believes the pattern of having many intimate relationships with boyfriends and girlfriends that frequently break up sets the stage for divorce later in life.

*"Why should the devil have all the good music?"*

—*Larry Norman, inventor of "Jesus Rock" music*

local public schools, while others fare poorly by comparison. Evangelical parents are hopeful that Christian schools will give their children better chances to make friends who share common values.

Some evangelical parents send their children into the public school system, and then talk with their children to find out what they are learning and discuss how this education fits with their faith. Some public high schools allow after-school Christian organizations such as Young Life or Bible study groups. Young Life has twenty-four youth camps across Canada and the United States where kids can go and enjoy a fun-filled week with a spiritual emphasis.

## CONTEMPORARY CHRISTIAN MUSIC

Contemporary Christian music (CCM) is a musical alternative begun by evangelicals, although its appeal has widened. Today, many people in the larger North American music scene enjoy listening to Christian artists. Groups and musicians such as Big Daddy Weave, BarlowGirl, Tree63, Casting Crowns, Point of Grace, and Steven Curtis Chapman are well known to evangelical teenagers.

CCM started in the 1960s and 1970s during the peace movement when young people across the United States had a spiritual revival known as the Jesus Movement. From this came a more culturally relevant or contemporary style of music. Over the years, CCM has evolved to include many styles of music such as jazz, rock, dance, blues, metal, alternative, New Age, rap, punk, grunge, industrial, thrash, and gothic. The music may sound the same as secular groups, but the words are about God and the Christian faith.

Evangelicals are surrounded by a culture that is often at odds with their deepest beliefs. Many see this as a risk to their children's spiritual well-being. Through prayerful parenting and church events, educational options like home schooling and Christian schools, and Christian music, many evangelical adults seek to guide the next generation into its own experience of evangelical faith.

# Chapter 6

RELIGION & MODERN CULTURE

## GOOD NEWS
## IN WORD & DEED

"All over this stadium, men and women are leaving their seats to come forward and accept Christ. What about you? Have you responded to Jesus Christ and taken him as your savior? This is your night. There are workers ready to pray with you now. Wherever you are sitting, just stand up and come forward. This is your opportunity to make life's most important decision."

The massive sports stadium is filled to capacity, but this is not a sports event. It is a Billy Graham Evangelistic Crusade. Thousands of people, of all different ages and races, have come this evening to hear the famous evangelist. There has been music by popular Christian musicians and preaching by Reverend Graham—all leading to this moment, the invitation to come forward and respond to Christ. Now, under the glow of the stadium lights, throngs of people make their way slowly down the aisles toward the stage on the field, while the choir softly sings the hymn "Just as I Am." The crowd gathers en masse, thousands of people sharing a moment of transition—their acceptance of the new birth.

Modern crusades such as this are more sophisticated versions of the revival services that originated in colonial times. They are based on the evangelical premise that each person needs to make a personal response to God. Billy Graham perfected this art of sharing the gospel with large crowds.

The Billy Graham Evangelistic Association (BGEA) exists "to support the evangelistic ministry and calling of Mr. Graham and to take the message of Christ to all we can by every *prudent* means available to us." Each year, the BGEA organizes a dozen crusades around the world. Keynote speakers are Billy Graham or his son Franklin. In 1992, Billy Graham announced that he was ill with Parkinson's disease and began slowing down his schedule. In June 2005, he led his last crusade meeting

Arranging a crusade involves much more than hiring a stadium, setting up the sound system, and flying the speakers to the event. Months before a crusade, the BGEA organizes help from hundreds of churches in the local community. Thousands of volunteers take classes on how to share the message of Christ and how to follow up with those who make the decision to accept Christ. In addition to crusades, the BGEA also produces television, radio and film shows, along with *Decision* magazine. The BGEA regularly publishes accurate information about all their finances; no hint of scandal has ever been associated with this organization.

# GLOSSARY

**guerrilla:** Member of a paramilitary unit, usually with some political objective such as the overthrow of a government.

**prudent:** Using good judgment to consider consequences and to act accordingly.

Public events are only one way evangelicals share the message of Christ with the world. They may also share the "good news" about Jesus by their words or by actions, in public events or one-on-one. Some evangelicals feel that showing God's love by helping others speaks more loudly than using their voices to proclaim God's love. As their name implies, evangelicals are committed to sharing the good news of Jesus Christ to all persons and by all means possible.

## WORLD VISION

On December 26, 2005, a tsunami devastated communities located on Asian coasts. Aceh, on the northern tip of Sumatra, was particularly hard hit. At least 1.8 million people in Aceh lost their homes or businesses. World Vision, an evangelical Christian relief organization, quickly responded to the need.

Within weeks, World Vision had provided food to more than 40,000 Aceh residents and supplied survival camping kits to almost six thousand. The organization began working on eighty temporary living centers (TLCs), each with twenty rooms, including schools and other vital services for residents whose homes and communities had been wiped out by the tsunami. The Aceh relief effort was only one of the numerous ministries sponsored by World Vision at that time.

Begun in 1950 by evangelical Bob Pierce as a response to the needs of Korean War orphans, today World Vision is one of the largest relief and development organizations in the world. It is currently involved with projects in more than ninety-nine nations. The organization sponsors two different kinds of projects. First, they provide short-term emergency response to disasters, such as the tsunami. These projects involve food, shelter, and medicine quickly provided to sustain lives. Second, they work with communities to develop agriculture, shelter, education, and small businesses that help communities avoid hunger or other disasters in the future. World Vision strives to be "child focused," realizing that children are the most vulnerable persons in communities threatened by hunger or disease. In 2003, World Vision raised $1.25 billion in donations that they used to serve 100 million people in ninety-nine countries. They also directly benefited 2.2 million children through a child sponsorship program.

Considering such huge numbers, it would be easy to overlook the fact that World Vision helps individuals—one at a time. Mohammad, a nine-year-old Indonesian boy, recalls the tidal wave that destroyed his community: "I saw the water coming. It looked like a big black wall. My mother picked me up, and we ran to the mosque." Though Mohammad and his mother survived, his father died. In March of 2005, Mohammad is slowly recovering. He spends each day at Child Friendly Space, a makeshift school and day-care center sponsored by World Vision. A teacher at the facility says the child struggles with grief, but "he is beginning to dream again."

## NEW TRIBES MISSION

Can you imagine what it would be like to grow up as the son or daughter of missionaries in the jungles of Paraguay? Your neighbors and playmates would be Manjui tribal members, who wear little clothing, live in palm-thatched huts, and live in isolation from the outside world. You would learn to hunt in jungles, catch a parrot or monkey for a pet, and speak a language that few people on earth have learned. At the same time, you would be hundreds of miles from a shopping mall or fast-food restaurant. Your parents would teach you and your siblings at home. If you had an emergency, a helicopter would fly out to evacuate you or drop needed supplies. You could really astonish your playmates by showing them movies on your DVD player; they have grown up without television or movies. On Sunday mornings, you would gather in an open-sided church, with almost a hundred tribal members who have become Christian in the past few years. If your family had not moved into the jungle, this church would not exist.

New Tribes Mission (NTM) is an evangelical organization that sends people into isolated regions of the world to live this challenging lifestyle. The organization is dedicated "to reaching people who have never had the opportunity to hear the Good News." NTM says there are approximately seven thousand cultural groups in the world, and of these, three thousand are "unreached" with the Christian message. NTM missionaries raise support from churches and friends to finance their lives in a tribal society. They leave their own culture and language, and spend years learning to understand and live among a tribal group where they translate the Bible into the tribal language, help villagers with practical needs (food, medicine, improved agriculture, and so on), and teach the Christian faith.

In the twenty-first century, some scholars and activists are critical of missionary efforts. Is it right to try to change people's traditional beliefs? Wouldn't tribal people be better off left alone? Evangelical

## A COUPLE WHO PAID THE ULTIMATE PRICE FOR THEIR FAITH

On their eighteenth wedding anniversary, Martin and Gracia Burnham received an unwelcome surprise. Abu Sayaff terrorists kidnapped the New Tribes missionaries to the Philippines while they were staying at Dos Palmas resort. While the Burnham's children returned to their home state of Kansas, Martin and Gracia endured more than a year of captivity in the jungle. They stayed true to their evangelical Christian beliefs. Martin offered to carry heavy packs—even for the terrorists—and spoke kindly to the man who chained him up every night. On the evening of June 7, 2002, Martin and Gracia said their prayers and went to sleep. Gunfire awakened them; the Philippine military was closing in on the terrorists. Martin died in the battle, and Gracia was wounded. Shortly before the battle, Martin told his wife, "We might not leave this jungle alive, but at least we can leave this world serving the Lord with gladness." Gracia Burnham wrote a book about their captivity, titled *In the Presence of My Enemies.*

missionaries respond that few if any tribal people will be left alone because loggers, **guerrilla** fighters, or miners will reach their villages. Evangelicals claim missionaries are more likely to help tribal people than these other groups. Missionaries point out how many lives they have saved by bringing medicine and technology to remote villages, and they say tribal people are more peaceful and happier after receiving the Christian message. Work among remote villages throughout the world is part of the evangelical belief that Jesus Christ died to bring men and women "from every tribe, nation, and language" into relationship with God.

## CANADIAN MENNONITES VOLUNTEER TO HELP IN THE WAKE OF DISASTER

Mennonite and Brethren, along with Quaker or Friends, are peace churches. Members of these religious groups belong to a tradition dating to the sixteenth century, are usually considered one type of evangelicals, and are pacifists—people who will not participate in war. Mennonite churches are especially common in Canada. The peace churches do an amazing amount of volunteer work, providing food, education, disaster relief, and other forms of aid to people around the world. When hurricanes ravaged Florida, when starvation hit Ethiopia, and when war caused destruction in Afghanistan, Mennonites provided relief and helped rebuild.

In Kamloops, British Columbia, twenty-three teenagers volunteered to help Mennonite Disaster Service (MDS) rebuild a home for a family stricken by fire. On their hands and knees, three teen volunteers sifted through ash searching for something precious that belonged to the owner of the burned home—her wedding ring. Incredibly, they found it! The three teens were "on cloud nine" according to their MDS supervisor.

## BRUCE WILKINSON FOLLOWS HIS DREAM

Bruce Wilkinson is an evangelical speaker and writer, founder of Walk Thru the Bible Ministries, and author of popular books *The Prayer of Jabez* and *The Dream Giver*. In *The Dream Giver*, Wilkinson encourages readers to "rise above the ordinary, conquer your fears, and overcome the obstacles that keep you from living your Big Dream."

Wilkinson follows his own advice. In 2002, he stepped down from Walk Thru the Bible Ministries. He says of that time, "I asked God what he wanted me to do next." Wilkinson sensed God leading him to do something big for Africans threatened by poverty, hunger, and illness. He formed Dream for Africa, a faith-based organization working for solutions to the hunger, orphans, and AIDS epidemic in sub-Saharan Africa. Wilkinson and his wife left their Georgia home and moved to South Africa. Dream for Africa had a vision of planting 100,000 gardens to feed 800,000 people by the end of 2004. Toward the end of the year, with just a few months to go, volunteers from around the world had already planted 96,000 gardens.

Wilkinson has a sober understanding of the dire needs in Africa. He says, "In Botswana, just three hours north of where we live, four out of every ten adults are dying of AIDS. Churches, agencies, and willing families in the region cannot keep up with the need." Nonetheless, Wilkinson believes there will be a miracle of caring response to the crisis in Africa. He encourages his readers, "You are called to go after larger and larger dreams for God." Wilkinson is living what he teaches—and helping many people in the process.

In 1995, evangelical scholar Alister McGrath made an optimistic pronouncement: "The Christian vision of the future now seems increasingly to belong to evangelicalism." At the same time, he warned, "Evangelicalism can never afford to take its . . . successes . . . for granted." A decade later, both of McGrath's statements ring true. Though evangelicals are the dominant religious group in the United States, they face several significant challenges in the near future.

Perhaps the most serious challenge facing the evangelical movement is that of youth. The majority of evangelical churchgoers are middle aged or older. Teen youth groups are popular, but a majority of young people leave church after they graduate from high school. Surveys show U.S. citizens in their twenties and thirties are unlikely to believe in the absolute authority of the Bible—a key evangelical belief. If evangelicals are to retain influence in North America, they must develop new ways to attract and keep young believers.

Another challenge is the role of women in evangelical churches. Some evangelicals understand the Bible as prohibiting women from leadership in churches, while others believe women can hold all the same offices as men. Traditionalists argue that feminism is a non-Christian philosophy harmful to God's standards of femininity and masculinity. Other evangelicals claim churches hinder themselves by limiting women's roles. The issue is emotional, and differences of opinion on the issue may hinder the evangelical movement.

A third challenge—but also an opportunity—is the increasing role of minority evangelicals in the United States and Canada. Vast numbers of Latinos are embracing pentecostal and charismatic faith. Numbers are tricky, but as many as ten million Latinos in the United States may affiliate with these groups. Chinese and Korean immigrants are also likely to worship as charismatics or evangelicals. Many black churches are evangelical in doctrine and practice, though they may not associate

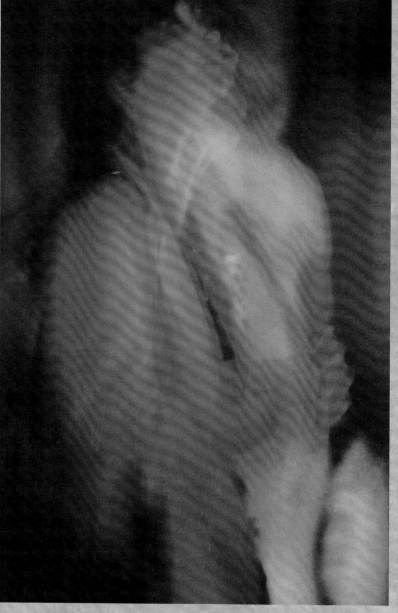

themselves with the evangelical movement. Evangelical churches are now common throughout the Navajo Nation. The challenge for evangelicals is incorporating these minority groups within networks so that they can work together for common causes. Evangelicals have repented of past racism, but they have not managed yet to form many effective partnerships across ethnic lines.

The role of homosexuals in church and society also challenges the evangelical movement. A majority of evangelicals believes that homosexual behaviors are not God's ideal way to live or that they are a sin. They correspondingly reject homosexuals as Christian leaders. Society judges the evangelical church as bigoted in this regard, yet the church is trying to be faithful to what it believes God has revealed in the Bible. Many evangelicals struggle for ways to remain faithful to their understanding of scripture while caring for homosexual relatives and friends.

The twenty-first century world differs markedly from that of the twentieth century. North Americans are more accepting of religious diversity and more willing to disagree with religious authorities. Some thinkers within the evangelical movement question whether evangelical beliefs are capable of answering the questions of the new century. Dave Tomlinson, who has coined the expression "post evangelical," suggests evangelicals need to question even their most treasured beliefs and consider whether these are relevant in today's world.

Brian McLaren raises similar questions. McLaren is the founding pastor of Cedar Ridge Community Church, a large church near Washington, D.C., that attracts many young believers. Like Tomlinson, McLaren suggests evangelicals may need to discard the labels and assumptions of the past. He urges them to move beyond an "us/them" way of thinking in order to embrace a broader definition of Christian faith. Other evangelicals are skeptical of the ideas proposed by Tomlinson and McLaren, believing traditional evangelical beliefs are vital to serve God effectively in the twenty-first century.

Will evangelicals continue to have a significant impact on North American society, or will they dwindle in numbers and influence over the coming years? Will evangelical beliefs change considerably in the coming decade, or will they remain constant? The future is uncertain. Yet evangelicals recall that Jesus promised his followers, "I am with you always, even to the end of the age" (Matthew 28:20). That promise continues to encourage and motivate evangelicals today.

Bakker, Jim. *I Was Wrong: The Untold Story of the Shocking Journey from PTL Power to Prison and Beyond.* Nashville, Tenn.: Thomas Nelson, 1996.

Bilezikian, Gilbert. *Christianity 101: Your Guide to Eight Basic Christian Beliefs.* Grand Rapids, Mich.: Zondervan, 1993.

Cymbala, Jim. *Fresh Wind, Fresh Fire: What Happens When God's Spirit Invades the Hearts of His People.* Grand Rapids, Mich.: Zondervan, 1997.

Epstein, Daniel Mark. *Sister Aimee: The Life of Aimee Semple McPherson.* Orlando, Fla.: Harcourt Brace & Company, 1993.

Strobel, Lee. *The Case for Christ: A Journalist's Personal Investigation of the Evidence for Jesus.* Grand Rapids, Mich.: Zondervan, 1998.

Wallis, Jim. *God's Politics: Why the Right Gets It Wrong and the Left Doesn't Get It.* New York: HarperCollins, 2005.

Warren, Rick. *The Purpose Driven Life: What on Earth Am I Here to Do?* Grand Rapids, Mich.: Zondervan, 2002.

Wilkinson, Bruce. *The Dream Giver.* Sisters, Ore.: Multnomah, 2003.

Williams, Peter W. *America's Religions: Traditions and Cultures.* New York: Macmillan, 1990.

# FOR MORE INFORMATION

The Barna Group
(research and surveys on evangelicals and other Christians)
www.barna.org

The Billy Graham Evangelistic
Association
www.billygraham.org

Campus Crusade for Christ
www.ccci.org

Joyce Meyer Ministries Official
Homepage
www.joycemeyer.org

New Tribes Mission
www.ntm.org

The Potter's Touch: T. D. Jakes
Ministries
www.tdjakes.org

Purpose Driven Life
www.purposedrivenlife.com

Reasons to Believe
www.reasons.org

Sojourners: Christians for Peace
and Justice
www.sojo.net

World Vision
www.WorldVision.org

Publisher's note:
The Web sites listed on this page were active at the time of publication. The publisher is not responsible for Web sites that have changed
their addresses or discontinued operation since the date of publication.
The publisher will review and update the Web-site list upon each
reprint.

# PICTURE CREDITS

The illustrations in RELIGION AND MODERN CULTURE are photo montages made by Dianne Hodack. They are a combination of her original mixed-media paintings and collages, the photography of Benjamin Stewart, various historical public-domain artwork, and other royalty-free photography collections.

AUTHORS:  Kenneth and Marsha McIntosh are former teachers. They have two children, Jonathan, nineteen, and Eirené, sixteen. Marsha has a bachelor's of science degree in Bible and education, and Kenneth has a bachelor's degree in English education and a master's degree in theology. They live in Flagstaff, Arizona, with their children, a dog, and two cats. Kenneth frequently speaks on topics of religion and society. Kenneth and Marsha have been involved in a variety of political causes over the past two decades.

CONSULTANT:  Dr. Marcus J. Borg is the Hundere Distinguished Professor of Religion and Culture in the Philosophy Department at Oregon State University. Dr. Borg is past president of the Anglican Association of Biblical Scholars. Internationally known as a biblical and Jesus scholar, the *New York Times* called him "a leading figure among this generation of Jesus scholars." He is the author of twelve books, which have been translated into eight languages. Among them are *The Heart of Christianity: Rediscovering a Life of Faith* (2003) and *Meeting Jesus Again for the First Time* (1994), the best-selling book by a contemporary Jesus scholar.

CONSULTANT:  Dr. Robert K. Johnston is Professor of Theology and Culture at Fuller Theological Seminary in Pasadena, California, having served previously as Provost of North Park University and as a faculty member of Western Kentucky University. The author or editor of thirteen books and twenty-five book chapters (including *The Christian at Play*, 1983; *The Variety of American Evangelicalism*, 1991; *Reel Spirituality: Theology and Film in Dialogue*, 2000; *Life Is Not Work/Work Is Not Life: Simple Reminders for Finding Balance in a 24/7 World*, 2000; *Finding God in the Movies: 33 Films of Reel Faith*, 2004; and *Useless Beauty: Ecclesiastes Through the Lens of Contemporary Film*, 2004), Johnston is the immediate past president of the American Theological Society, an ordained Protestant minister, and an avid bodysurfer.